W9-BHI-576

Ripley's Believe It or Not!®

Developed and produced by Ripley Publishing Ltd

This edition published and distributed by:

Mason Crest
450 Parkway Drive, Suite D, Broomall, PA 19008
www.masoncrest.com

Printed and bound in the United States of America

First printing
9 8 7 6 5 4 3 2 1

Ripley's Believe It or Not!
Awesome Arts
ISBN: 978-1-4222-3148-7 (hardback)
Ripley's Believe It or Not!—Complete 8 Title Series
ISBN: 978-1-4222-3147-0

Cataloging-in-Publication Data on file with the Library of Congress

PUBLISHER'S NOTE
While every effort has been made to verify the accuracy of the entries in this book, the
Publishers cannot be held responsible for any errors contained in the work. They would
be glad to receive any information from readers.

WARNING
Some of the stunts and activities in this book are undertaken by experts and should not
be attempted by anyone without adequate training and supervision.

Download The Weird

AWESOME ARTS

www.MasonCrest.com

Flying House

Inspired by the Disney/Pixar movie *Up*, a house took to the sky near Los Angeles, California, attached to 300 weather balloons, setting a new world record for the largest balloon cluster flight. The 18-ft-high (5.5-m), custom-built, lightweight house was re-created by engineers from *National Geographic* and, with the balloons on top, stood ten stories high. It flew for about an hour, reaching an altitude of 10,000 ft (3,000 m). To lift an average-sized, normal-weight house off the ground would actually require more than 20 million helium balloons.

UP IS THE ONLY BEST PICTURE OSCAR NOMINEE TO HAVE JUST TWO LETTERS IN ITS TITLE.

R WAND DAMAGE During the making of the eight Harry Potter movies, actor Daniel Radcliffe (who plays the boy wizard) got through 160 pairs of glasses and wore out nearly 70 wands.

R LONG WAIT U.S. actress Romola Remus Dunlap (1900–1987), the first actress to portray *The Wizard of Oz* character Dorothy Gale in film, has only two film credits and they are 77 years apart—1908 and 1985.

R SMOKIN' GUITARS Chuck Meyer of New Lenox, Illinois, builds guitars and mandolins from cigar boxes, and spends hours searching flea markets, tobacco shops, and eBay for boxes that will give the best sound.

R SALSA SENSATION U.K. salsa dancer Sarah Jones won Spain's *You've Got Talent* TV show in 2009—at the age of 75. She won the first prize for an acrobatic routine with her dancing partner Nicko, 40 years her junior.

The Blair Witch Project

Rear Window

Guitar Revenge

Japanese artist Yoshihiko Satoh has designed 12-necked guitars that are almost impossible to play. After fretting over his own inability to learn the guitar, he decided to create 72-string monsters that even the most accomplished musician would struggle to play. Each guitar took up to six months to make and some have sold for $90,000.

YOUNG REPORTER As Hurricane Irene battered the U.S. East Coast on August 27, 2011, five-year-old Jane Haubrich from Doylestown, Pennsylvania, became the world's youngest TV reporter by delivering regular weather updates throughout the day via CNN's iReport. Her last report was sent over right before her bedtime.

FAMOUS POSE In 1928, Mexican actor Emilio Fernández was approached by Hollywood art director Cedric Gibbons to pose naked for a full-length sketch. Fernandez agreed reluctantly, but the moment made him immortal as the drawing was used to create the design for the Oscar statuette.

COOL MOVIES A temporary outdoor movie theater in London, England, was built mainly from 150 recycled refrigerators. U.S. design student Lindsey Scannapieco conceived "Films on Fridges," a venue where the screen was surrounded by old fridges, the bar was made of fridge parts, and fridge doors were incorporated into the seating.

PARTY POOPER In their teens, the Followill brothers of U.S. rock band Kings of Leon used to throw parties at their father Ivan's house. When Ivan decided it was time for the party to break up, he would put jalapenos in the microwave, and the fumes burned everyone's eyes so that they quickly left the house.

ORGAN RECITAL Fueled by coffee, vitamins, and jellybeans, Jacqueline Sadler of Toronto, Canada, played a church organ continuously for over 40 hours in June 2011.

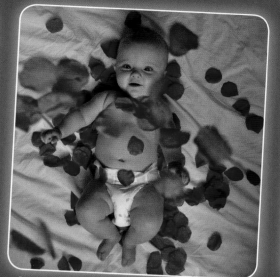
American Beauty

HERE'S LOOKING AT YOU, KID

A six-month-old baby has attracted 50,000 hits a month on his Internet blog by posing with props for pictures that re-create classic movie scenes. With the help of his mother Emily and assorted stuffed toys, Arthur Hammond from Oxford, England, has conjured up iconic images from movies including *Rambo: First Blood, American Beauty, The Blair Witch Project, Jaws, Alien,* and *The Godfather*.

Rambo: First Blood

R DELAYED DOCTORATE Queen guitarist Brian May has a PhD in astrophysics. He completed his thesis on interplanetary dust clouds at Imperial College, London, England, in 2007—36 years after he started, having postponed his doctorate in favor of a career as a rock star.

R TWO FUNERALS A month after Michael Jackson died in 2009, a ceremonial funeral was held for him—without the body—in the Ivory Coast village of Krindjabo, where he was crowned a prince of the Agni people while on a visit to the country in 1992.

R TOP TOUR U2's 360° Tour (2009–11) grossed $736 million in ticket sales, making it the highest-grossing concert tour of all time. With 120 trucks needed to transport each of the three giant claw sets, the tour cost over $750,000 a day to stage.

R VIVID DREAM Released by the Beatles in 1965, Paul McCartney's "Yesterday" has since been covered more than 1,600 times, making it the most recorded song in modern music history. McCartney composed the entire melody in a dream one night and before writing the final lyrics he gave it the working title "Scrambled Eggs."

R COMIC COLLECTION Brett Chilman of Henley Brook, Western Australia, has been collecting comic books for over 30 years and now has more than 68,000. His comics are stored in two houses and are worth an estimated $1.3 million.

R GRENADE ATTACK The band La Excelencia was attacked with guns and a grenade—killing two band members—for refusing to play an encore performance after a set in Guadalajara, Mexico, on January 17, 2011.

Before
After

SUPERMAN'S DOUBLE

Superman fanatic Herbert Chavez, from Calamba City in the Philippines, has undergone more than 13 years of cosmetic surgery to make him look like the comic-book hero. His nose has been reshaped, he has had a chin augmentation to acquire Superman's iconic cleft, silicone injections in his lips to make them fuller, liposuction on his stomach, and thigh implants to make his legs appear more muscular. As he is only 5 ft 6 in (1.67 m) and Superman is 6 ft 2 in (1.88 m), Herbert says: "I wouldn't rule out surgery to make me taller."

Creature Feature

Andrew Lancaster is an unusually inventive taxidermist from New Zealand. He has turned the traditional skill on its head with his bizarre mutant creations, stitching different dead animals together to make creepy new creatures. Lancaster, an ex-farmer who has been into taxidermy for 14 years, regularly stops his car to pick up roadkill for his projects. Although his pieces might look outrageous, they are made using traditional techniques, taking a few hours to complete before they are dried out over a period of two weeks.

This creature features a possum's body and a doll's head.

☒ YOUNG PAINTER At age four, Aelita Andre of Melbourne, Australia, had a solo art exhibition at a gallery in New York City—and her paintings sold for up to $9,000 each. Aelita, who has been painting since she was just 11 months old, specializes in large, colorful, abstract works, which often have children's toys and other small objects stuck to them.

☒ UNDERWEAR EXHIBIT Yi Ci, a student at China's Hubei Institute of Fine Arts, collected several hundred items of underwear to arrange as a piece of art entitled *Privacy* for her graduation exhibition.

☒ BRICK CAR Chinese artist Dai Geng spent over a year making a full-sized model of a BMW car by cementing hundreds of bricks together. Only the windows of the car are not made of brick. The bodywork, tires, steering wheel, exhaust pipe, and trimmings are all brick, and he even managed to build brick hinges so that the doors open and close.

☒ FOOD ILLUSTRATOR Graphic designer David Meldrum from Essex, England, kept a record of everything he ate for a year between June 15, 2010, and June 14, 2011, by painting every meal. His illustrations, which were exhibited at a London gallery, revealed that in the course of the 12 months he consumed 1,360 cups of coffee, 305 pints of Peroni beer, and 122 Freddo chocolate bars.

☒ LONGEST TRAIN In 2011, after more than 3,500 hours of work, a group of volunteers from Wilmington Railroad Museum, North Carolina, built a model train comprising 31 locomotives and 1,563 freight cars that stretched a record 925 ft (282 m) long, and could move under its own power.

☒ TOOTHPICK LINER Wayne Kusy used a million toothpicks to make a model of the liner *Queen Mary* that was so big it filled his Chicago, Illinois, apartment. The 25-ft-long (7.6-m) model had to be built in six sections so that he could get it out of the building.

☒ MASTER FORGER For decades, experts believed that *The Procuress*, a painting at the Courtauld Institute of Art in London, England, was a prized 17th-century copy of a work by Dutch master Dirck van Baburen. However, in 2011 it emerged that the painting was instead the work of Dutch master forger Han van Meegeren, who died in 1947. Van Meegeren, who specialized in faking great artworks, swindled his buyers out of the equivalent of $100 million in today's money. One forgery fooled the Rijksmuseum in Amsterdam into parting with the equivalent of $18 million, but that painting now languishes in the museum storeroom.

WORLD'S SMALLEST ENGRAVING

In February 2011, after eight months' work, Graham Short of Birmingham, England, completed the world's smallest engraving by human hand. He engraved the motto "Nothing is impossible," measuring just 39/1000 in (0.1 mm), on the edge of a razor blade, the letters being so tiny that they can only be read with the aid of a microscope set at 400-times magnification. He was only able to work at night when there was no vibration from traffic, and did so with his right arm strapped to the arm of his chair to minimize movement. To ensure his body was perfectly still, he used a stethoscope to monitor his heart, and tried to make a stroke of a letter only between heartbeats. Even so, it took him around 150 attempts before he was able to complete the artwork, which later went on sale for £47,500.

ALI TRIBUTE

Californian artist Michael Kalish created a giant tribute to boxer Muhammad Ali out of 1,300 punch bags. Viewed close up, the 26 x 23 x 25 ft (7.9 x 7 x 7.6 m) installation, which was unveiled in Nokia Plaza, Los Angeles, in March 2011, looks like a series of punch bags randomly hung from a metal frame. It's only from a distance that the punch bags morph into a portrait of Ali.

Bruce Springsteen

WEIRDEST
BACKSTAGE RIDERS

When singers and rock bands reach the top they demand some strange things backstage, before and after performing.

VAN HALEN Van Halen demanded a candy bowl of M&M's with the brown sweets picked out and discarded.

AC/DC In 2008, the "Highway To Hell" rockers required the promoter to make sure that three oxygen tanks and three oxygen masks be made available at the U.S. venues they were playing. Additionally, Twinings English Breakfast Tea and a case of bottled beer were two of their less demanding needs.

THE ROLLING STONES On the Stones' 1997–98 Bridges To Babylon tour rider was a request for a full-sized snooker table (a pool table would not be acceptable) and the necessary accessories, such as cues and chalk. Bizarrely, the band's rider also mentioned that the tour organizers would be providing their own balls.

CHRISTINA AGUILERA A police escort, a large vanity mirror, dressing room plants and flowers, four candles and matches, and the rider staple, honey, are just a few of the demands on Christina Aguilera's four-page tour document from 2000.

BRUCE SPRINGSTEEN Sensibly, "The Boss" likes to have a designated guitar security guard watch over his precious guitar at all times and practical backstage supplies of protein and energy-enhancing products.

50 CENT An all-day supply of peanut-butter-and-jelly sandwiches is what rapper 50 Cent needed to perform to the maximum. Chewing gum and cough drops were also essentials on his 2005 backstage shopping list, together with shrimps on ice.

7 ROCK STARS
who caught fire on stage

Michael Jackson—Firework malfunction Jackson was filming a Pepsi commercial in 1984 when a firework display behind him malfunctioned, showering his head with sparks, which set fire to his hair. With audience members wrongly thinking it was all part of the act, Jackson calmly covered his head with his jacket while his brothers rushed to his aid. He suffered second-degree burns and wore a hairpiece when collecting his Grammy awards later that year.

Gene Simmons—Fire-breather The frontman of U.S. band KISS wows the crowds by filling his mouth with kerosene before blowing it out over a flame to create a huge fireball. He has caught fire more than a dozen times doing it, but fortunately one of the crew is always on hand with a wet towel.

James Hetfield—Stepped into shooting flame The frontman of U.S. rock band Metallica was performing before 55,000 fans at Montréal's Olympic Stadium in 1992 when he accidentally stepped into the path of one of the 12-ft-high (3.6-m) special-effects flames that had been rigged to shoot up from the front of the stage. His guitar protected him from the full force of the 3,200°F (1,760°C) blast, but fire still engulfed his left side, searing his hand and arm, burning off his eyebrows, and singeing his face and hair. Despite suffering second- and third-degree burns, he was back on stage 17 days later.

27 AN UNLUCKY NUMBER FOR ROCK LEGENDS

They didn't all sell their souls to the devil, as legend has it bluesman Robert Johnson did when just 27. So let's just hope it's nothing more than weird coincidence that links all these top music makers who died at that tragically early age. The dearly departed list of seven that died young is...

1911–1938 Robert Johnson died aged 27 years and three months

1942–1969 Brian Jones The Rolling Stones' guitarist, died aged 27 years and four months

1942–1970 Jimi Hendrix died aged 27 years and nine months

1943–1970 Janis Joplin died aged 27 years and eight months

1943–1971 Jim Morrison lead singer with The Doors, died aged 27 years and seven months

1967–1994 Kurt Cobain lead singer with Nirvana, died aged 27 years and one month

Amy Winel...

Vomit Artist

DEATH WATCH BEETLE Artist Mike Libby from Portland, Oregon, customizes real dead insects, spiders, and crabs with antique watch parts and electronic components to create intricate sculptures of new hybrid creatures. He was inspired by finding an intact dead beetle, which he thought looked and worked like a small mechanical device. So, he sought out an old wristwatch, and added its screws, springs, and gears to the insect's body to create a mechanical beetle sculpture. Each of his pieces takes up to 40 hours to create and can sell for up to $2,000.

SUSHI SOCCER In August 2011, 20 chefs in Bodø, Norway, created a soccer-themed mosaic from 13,000 pieces of sushi over an area of 270 sq ft (25 sq m).

PICASSO'S FIRST WORD WAS "LAPIZ," WHICH IS SPANISH FOR PENCIL.

WORKING MODEL Fernando Benavides from Madrid, Spain, has built a remote-control LEGO® car that has all-wheel drive, a working seven-speed dual-clutch transmission, a working retractable hardtop, a retractable spoiler, and three working differentials. He spent 18 months building the Porsche 911 Cabriolet from 3,500 LEGO® parts.

MARBLE MOSAIC A team of 15 artists from the U.K. and Bahrain spent four months creating a marble mosaic of the Sultan of Oman using 128,274 individual pieces of marble in 90 different natural shades. The mosaic measured 27.2 ft x 17.4 ft (8.3 x 5.3 m) and had to be created using a photograph of the sultan, as he rarely appears in public and did not sit for the artwork in person. His face alone took 40 days to complete, the beard and mustache being made from the sultan's favorite stone, imported all the way from Italy.

LABOR OF LOVE Despite losing the sight in her left eye when she was a child, 69-year-old grandmother Heather Hems, of Hampshire, England, has spent 12 hours a day for more than 17 years creating an embroidery covering 540 sq ft (50 sq m)—the size of 12 table tennis tables. Her creation features important world figures, as well as major global events such as the Moon landing. She has devoted more than 70,000 hours to the tapestry, spending thousands of dollars on materials. The work has also been so physically exhausting that she has had to undergo shoulder surgery.

ARTIFICIAL ANIMALS Dutch artist Theo Jansen creates giant artificial animals from plastic pipes and rubber tubes that walk around powered by wind and carry sensors that allow them to change direction. One of his kinetic creatures is so sophisticated that it can anchor itself to the ground if it senses a storm approaching.

ANTLER STATUE Artist Kurt Gordon of Dubois, Wyoming, created a life-sized elk statue made entirely of discarded antlers. Gordon, who has been working with antlers for over 35 years, has also sold antler chandeliers to hotels all over the world.

ON TAPE Ukrainian-born Mark Khaisman from Philadelphia, Pennsylvania, creates amazing artworks—including his favorite movie scenes—from packing tape. By using layers of translucent brown tape on backlit Plexiglas panels, he is able to depict light and shade and even detailed facial features. The darkest sections of his images require up to ten layers of tape, and he uses around three 330-ft (100-m) rolls on each picture.

POST-IT® DRAWINGS Artist John Kenn Mortensen of Copenhagen, Denmark, has drawn over 250 illustrations on humble Post-it Notes. His works, which sell for up to $100 each, often feature spooks and creatures inspired by U.S. horror author Stephen King.

BECOMING VINCENT Artist James Birbeck from Edmonton, Canada, turned himself into a Vincent van Gogh portrait. After friends noted his physical resemblance to the Dutch master, Birbeck bought a jacket like Vincent's and applied paints and makeup to his face to complete the transformation.

FOOT CARVER Pema Tshering of Thimphu, Bhutan, is a professional artist who carves and paints with his feet. He was born with cerebral palsy and congenital deformities in his spinal column, which have rendered both of his arms useless. He also has only limited use of his legs, but carves beautiful wooden dragons, holding the implements between his toes.

Ripley's ask

The Ripley's Believe It or Not! team met up with Millie Brown to find out why and how she creates vomit art…

Millie, you create works of art from the unique medium of vomit—how do you do it? Well, it's a long process that involves drinking dyed soy milk at intervals—one color at a time. I then vomit onto the canvas, pausing between colors so that they retain their true colors and don't mix together.

How difficult is it to get the paint where you want it to go on the canvas? I often have a pattern in mind but also let it take its own direction, depending on the mood, you can never fully control it. But that's what I like about the whole process, it makes every piece completely unique.

Do you need recovery time before you paint again? I once did a performance where I vomited the whole rainbow, and I don't think I could do that every day. I usually leave a month between performances, so I have enough recovery time.

Does vomiting as often as you do affect your health at all? Not really. I am extremely healthy in every other way. I am a vegan and am very into nutrition. My performance clearly isn't very good for me, but I think my overall healthy lifestyle the rest of the time balances it all out.

You collaborated with Lady Gaga—how did that come about? Lady Gaga was doing her "Monster Ball Interlude" film with Nick Knight and Ruth Hogben for her Monster Ball Tour when she called me and asked me to vomit on her dress. The video was used as a backdrop throughout the tour. It was amazing to see it projected on huge screens and to hear the crowd's reaction to it.

Is there a particular statement you are making in your work? I think it is far more interesting to let people make their own decisions about it. I always find that it means something different to each person.

Turn the page

Vomit Artist

Millie Brown creates unique works of art by vomiting. Mastering the ability to regurgitate different colors to order, she has established herself as an international "Vomit Artist," and in 2010 even threw up over Lady Gaga's dress for the singer's Monster Ball Tour interlude.

Millie, from London, England, first performed her "vomit art" live at a 2006 art show in Berlin—a daunting feat as she had never made herself sick before and had no idea whether she could.

Vomiting may seem a random exercise, but Millie has got it down to a fine art. First she makes sure that she does not eat for two days before a performance. Then she mixes soy milk with different color food dyes to create the palette she would like for the piece. Next she sits down and slowly drinks the milk before approaching the blank canvas. There, she stands up or kneels down and begins to make herself sick by sticking her fingers down her throat, and, almost without noise, vomits onto the canvas.

Fountains of colorful vomit fly from her mouth and splash onto the canvas, leaving bits of it dripping from her hands and face. After she has completed the first color, she vomits some more offstage to make sure all of that color is flushed out of her body. Then the process starts over again with colors number two, three, and four.

One of Millie's artworks sold for $2,400, and when she performed exclusively for *Ripley's Believe It or Not!* she stunned the team with her beautiful, yet bizarre, show. Ripley's has since acquired the final piece for display at one of the *Ripley's Believe It or Not!* museums around the world.

Millie uses her fingers to make herself sick and then vomits colored soy milk onto the canvas

Millie's finished work of art

Nipple Dress

At the 2011 London Fashion Week, Liverpool designer Rachael Freire unveiled a rose-covered dress made of 3,000 real cow nipples. Created from patches of leather recovered from tanneries, the dress was part of her *Nippleocalypse* collection, which also featured a bra made from layers of protruding nipples.

▣ POPPED THE QUESTION For her wedding to Duncan Turner, schoolteacher Rachel Robinson from Lincolnshire, England, wore a dress made from bubble wrap. The dress and train were made out of 13 ft (4 m) of the packing material by pupils and parents from her school. The sheets of bubble wrap were stitched together, attached to an inner lining of cloth, and topped off with white packing foam and candies.

▣ SHORT STORIES A 2005 anthology of fiction called *Meeting Across the River* comprised 20 short stories by different writers based entirely on a song of the same title from the 1975 Bruce Springsteen album *Born To Run*.

▣ UNWASHED JEANS Josh Le, a student at the University of Alberta in Edmonton, Canada, wore the same pair of jeans nearly every day for 15 months without washing them. At the end of the experiment, he found that the amount of bacteria on his unwashed jeans was no greater than on a pair that had been worn for only 13 days.

▣ MUSICAL TIE British Conservative Member of Parliament Nadhim Zahawi apologized to fellow members during a debate in the House of Commons after he was interrupted in the middle of a speech by his own musical tie. The red tie emitted a tinny tune that was amplified by a microphone above his head.

▣ RECORD RUN Actor George Lee Andrews played opera house-manager Monsieur André in the same Broadway production of the musical *Phantom of the Opera* for 23 years and a record 9,382 shows. During his run, 12 different actors played the role of the Phantom.

CHART GLEE In 2010, the cast of the TV series *Glee* had 80 singles chart on the Billboard Hot 100, the most by any act in a single year in the chart's history.

AUTO ACCIDENT Dutch TV show host Ruben Nicolai was run over while recording a 2011 show designed to find the country's worst driver. The driver was performing a task that involved steering between traffic cones when he lost control and sent the car careering toward a cameraman and Nicolai, who was taken to hospital with a torn lip, shoulder pain, and a sore foot.

SHED GIGS Jon Earl has used his garden shed, measuring just 12 x 10 ft (3.6 x 3 m), in Somerset, England, to stage gigs by more than 1,000 musicians from all over the world, including legendary folk-rock band Fairport Convention and a 26-strong gospel choir.

TOTAL FAITH Hollywood executives were apprehensive about casting Leonardo DiCaprio as the Kid in the 1995 movie *The Quick and the Dead*, but co-star Sharon Stone was so confident in his ability she paid his salary out of her own pocket.

INTERVIEW KING From every U.S. president since Gerald Ford to rap star Snoop Dogg, TV host Larry King has interviewed more than 50,000 people in a career spanning over 50 years. That works out at an average of more than three interviews a day.

TV WATCHDOGS Recent research shows that the average dog in the U.K. watches 50 minutes of TV a day, with one in ten watching at least two hours. Labradors are the biggest TV addicts and soaps are dogs' favorite programs.

SQUARE EYES

To mark the 60th anniversary of TV in the Netherlands, six people stayed awake and watched TV nonstop for 87 hours. Fifty-five people started out in the attempt—staged in pods at a studio in Hilversum—but by the fourth evening only six were still glued to their screen.

QUEEN DETHRONED In January 1976, Queen's song "Bohemian Rhapsody," which contains the famous line "mamma mia, mamma mia, mamma mia, let me go," was knocked off the number one spot in the U.K. chart by Abba's "Mamma Mia."

MINIATURE MOVIE SCENES

Spanish artist Maya Pixelskaya has carefully re-created scenes from her favorite movies such as *Jaws*, *Amélie*, and *The Wicker Man*—on her fingernails. For each miniature painting, she applies a layer of white nail polish and draws over it with a tiny marker pen to create the basic outline. She then applies up to six layers of nail polish, and because she needs to let each layer dry before proceeding to the next, she has to keep her fingers still for hours on end.

TOAST OF HOLLYWOOD Screen legend Marilyn Monroe has been immortalized in Shanghai, China, in the form of a huge toast portrait by New Zealand artist Maurice Bennett, measuring 13 x 12 ft (4 x 3.6 m) and comprising almost 6,000 slices of bread.

BULLET NECKLACE Lovetta Conto, a teenage artist from Liberia, uses disarmed ammunition from her country's 1999–2003 Civil War to make jewelry. Her handcrafted necklaces of spent bullet casings have been worn by the likes of Halle Berry and Angelina Jolie.

LIVING PAINTINGS When Washington, D.C., artist Alexa Meade paints her subjects, she really does paint them. Instead of using a canvas, she paints directly on to the bodies of her models with acrylic paints, making the 3-D subjects appear 2-D. Only the eyes and hair are left untouched. She then photographs the result, which looks uncannily like a conventional painting hanging in a gallery.

SMILEY FACE At Continental Soldier's Park in Mahwah, New Jersey, 2,226 people wearing yellow ponchos gathered to create a huge human-made smiley face.

CART TREES For the 2010 holiday season, Anthony Schmitt of Santa Monica, California, built two giant Christmas-tree statues using 86 shopping carts. The trees, which went on display in his home city and in Emeryville, California, had full-sized carts at the base and smaller ones on the top, all the carts being supported by an internal structure.

FREEHAND CIRCLE Alex Overwijk, a math teacher from Ottawa, Ontario, Canada, can draw a perfect freehand circle about 3 ft (1 m) in diameter in less than a second—and the YouTube clip showing him performing the feat has attracted more than six million hits.

Light Paintings

Scary skeletons with brightly illuminated bones rising menacingly up through the trees make the snow-covered woods of Finland seem really spooky. These light-painting photographs are the work of Helsinki artist Janne Parviainen who creates them by using different light sources during varying exposure times, ranging from a few seconds to several hours. While the camera is exposing, his skeletons and other figures are drawn with LED lights.

Janne's light "mummies" appear in an eerie movie theater—complete with popcorn.

Janne places his skeletons in everyday situations as well as scary ones, as this cool guitarist demonstrates.

SQUARE HOLE In June 2011, what appeared to be a giant hole opened up in the middle of the main square in Stockholm, Sweden—but it turned out to be an imaginative work of photographic art. The 3-D optical illusion, measuring 105 x 59 ft (32 x 18 m), was created by Swedish artist Erik Johansson.

GIANT SHOE A giant shoe measuring 18 ft (5.5 m) long was unveiled in Amsterdam, the Netherlands, in November 2010. The shoe was an exact replica of a Converse Chuck Taylor All Star—and was equivalent to a U.S. size 845.

INSTANT CAMERAS Wong Ting Man of Hong Kong, China, owns more than 1,000 instant cameras—including more than 800 Polaroids—at an estimated value of $130,000.

STAR WARS MOSAIC Hungarian artist Zoltán Simon designed a *Star Wars* mosaic in London, England, in 2011 that covered 1,050 sq ft (97.5 sq m) and was made up of 384,000 LEGO® bricks.

BALLOON SCULPTURE New York artist Larry Moss used balloons to re-create scenes from children's fairy tales, such as *Rapunzel*, *The Frog Prince*, and *The Three Little Pigs*. He was even able to build a balloon beanstalk strong enough to support a real child to depict *Jack and the Beanstalk*. He started working with balloons more than 25 years ago, and his previous artworks have included a balloon *Mona Lisa* and four haunted houses, each made from 100,000 balloons.

MAGGOT ART Rebecca O'Flaherty, an entomologist at the University of California, creates "Maggot Art" from colored trails left by maggots that have been dipped in paint. Using special larval forceps, she dips the squirming maggots in brightly colored, nontoxic, water-based paint, places them on a sheet of paper and watches them crawl.

SOLE SIGNATURE Considered to be one of the greatest artists of all time, Italian Renaissance painter and sculptor Michelangelo (1475–1564) signed only one of his many sculptures during his entire artistic career.

PAINTS WITH TOES Despite being born without hands, Zohreh Etezad Saltaneh of Tehran, Iran, paints so beautifully with her feet that her artworks have been shown in more than 60 exhibitions around the world. Her mother placed a paintbrush between Zohreh's toes when she was young to encourage her painting. She has also learned to weave intricate Persian carpets using her toes.

PICASSO IN WOOL A group of 40 women called The Materialistics, from Tyne and Wear, England, spent months knitting copies of famous works of art. They began by drawing the image of the original artwork on graph paper and then applied a yarn finish to pieces such as *The Scream* by Edvard Munch, *Seated Woman in Garden* by Pablo Picasso, and *Sunflowers* by Vincent van Gogh.

GIANT COIN Wander Martich of Grand Rapids, Michigan, made a giant replica of a 1-cent coin from 84,000 pennies. Working more than ten hours a day for three months, she glued each penny onto a 10-ft-high (3-m) wooden frame. She used the different natural shades of pennies to create the image and traded in some old coins for shiny new ones from the U.S. Mint to form the highlights. Ripley's saw the coin at an art show and have since acquired it for display in one of its museums.

Bodies appear to lie immobile in the snow with footprints of light walking away into the distance.

TIME KEEPER During the making of the 1963 movie *Cleopatra*, Elizabeth Taylor's then husband Eddie Fisher was paid $1,500 a day just to make sure she got to work on time.

MINIATURE MASTERPIECE Collector of miniature books Nikunj Vagadia of Rajkot, India, owns a tiny gold-plated copy of Mahatma Gandhi's autobiography that measures a mere 1.3 x 1.8 in (3.25 x 4.5 cm).

DEAF RAPPER Sean Forbes of Detroit, Michigan, has been deaf since childhood—yet he is a professional musician and rapper who uses sign language for each lyric as he speaks it.

ONE TITLE To boost sales of his 2011 book *Martian Summer: Robot Arms, Cowboy Spacemen, and My 90 Days with the Phoenix Mars Mission*, Brooklyn author Andrew Kessler opened a new bookstore in New York City's West Village and stocked it with 3,000 copies of just one book—his own. The store, Ed's Martian Book, had alien artwork on the walls and was divided into sections including "staff favorite," "self-help," and "best seller," although in each case the recommendation was, of course, the same book.

BOSS TRIBUTE There are more than 60 Bruce Springsteen tribute acts working in the United States and Europe, including The B Street Band who played at New Jersey governor Chris Christie's inaugural ball after Springsteen himself declined the invitation.

RARE FIND Members of the St. Laurence Church in the village of Hilmarton in Wiltshire, England, found a 400-year-old original copy of the 1611 King James Bible, of which fewer than 200 exist, sitting unnoticed on a church shelf.

ENCYCLOPEDIA GIGANTICA

Connecticut-based British designer Rob Matthews had a novel idea to highlight how much we rely on cyberspace for information—he published a book made from hundreds of articles from the popular Wikipedia website, and it's 19 in (48 cm) thick. Incredibly, Rob used only 437 articles from the site, just 0.002 percent of the content available. If all the articles on Wikipedia were made into a book, it would be over 225 million pages long, or 13½ mi (21.6 km) thick, and would require a bookshelf the length of Manhattan Island in New York.

NUMBERS BOOK *A Million Random Digits with 100,000 Normal Deviates*, a book containing nothing but a giant list of randomly generated numbers, sold thousands of copies in the 1950s and 1960s.

HUMAN ROBOT Wang Kang, a telecoms worker from Shanghai, China, enjoyed the 2008 movie *Iron Man* so much that he spent nearly three years building his own 110-lb (50-kg) suit of armor and then wore it to the office—to the amazement of his work colleagues. Some froze as he approached them in his robotic suit, and others screamed.

HEALTHY PROFIT Leafing through a pile of old textbooks bought at an auction in 2010 for a total of $10, Bill and Cindy Farnsworth of Austin, Texas, found a 25-cent banknote that had been hand-signed in 1843 by the President of the Republic of Texas, Sam Houston. They later sold the note for $63,250.

BEST SELLERS With combined sales of more than 450 million copies (and translated into 67 languages), J.K. Rowling's series of Harry Potter books is the fourth best seller of all time, behind only the Bible (3 billion copies), the Quran (1.5 billion), and *Quotations from Chairman Mao* (800 million).

CLOWNING AROUND

A bizarre fashion craze swept Mexico in 2011, with young men sporting flamboyant cowboy-style boots with curled toes, some measuring more than 3 ft (1 m) long. The footwear epidemic originated in the town of Matehuala, where a shoemaker was asked by a mysterious customer if he could make him a pair of boots with elongated toes that curved upward. Dancers at local rodeo nightclubs picked up on the impractical fashion accessory and soon the boots had spread to nearby towns and even across the border into the United States. The stretched shoes created such a buzz that people made their own extensions at home, adding flashing lights and glitter.

EUROPE TOUR London, England, music journalist Greg Parmley visited 26 live music festivals across Europe in 30 days. Traveling by motorbike, he journeyed 5,500 mi (8,800 km) through 13 countries and saw over 150 bands playing live.

ENTERPRISING MANUAL In 2010, Haynes, the U.K. publisher best known for its in-depth car manuals, unveiled an unusual addition to its range of workshop titles—a detailed guidebook devoted to the workings of *Star Trek's* U.S.S. *Enterprise*.

Smurf Alert

For the launch of the 2011 Sony Picture movie *The Smurfs*, the traditional white houses, businesses, and even a church in the Spanish village of Júzcar were painted blue, using 1,110 gal (4,200 l) of paint. The locals liked the new color so much they voted to keep it. For the film itself, designers built an exact two-thirds replica of Belvedere Castle in Central Park, New York.

R TWIST PARADE During the 2011 Mandan Independence Day Parade in Mandan, North Dakota, 2,158 people lined up on Main Street to dance the Twist.

R ELVIS FESTIVAL Over 4,000 Elvis Presley fans flock to the annual Elvis Festival at Collingwood, Ontario, Canada, which ends with over 120 Elvis impersonators competing to become Grand Champion.

R ELEPHANT ORCHESTRA Formed by U.S. composer Dave Soldier and conservationist Richard Lair, the Thai Elephant Orchestra has released three CDs of music, which feature elephants playing giant instruments such as xylophones, drums, and harmonicas.

R ELVIS IMPERSONATOR Simon Goldsmith of Suffolk, England, sang Elvis Presley hits nonstop for more than 35 hours in 2010.

R FAMOUS WIGGLE The bottom wiggle that became one of Marilyn Monroe's trademarks was the result of her having weak ankles and bow legs. Once she saw the attention her walk was getting, she emphasized it by sawing a quarter of an inch off the right heel of all of her shoes.

R FIRST NOVEL A girl with cerebral palsy who can write only by touching a keyboard with her lips has been offered a contract to have her first novel published. Wang Qianjin, 18, of Zhenjiang, China, is virtually completely paralyzed and has never had a day's schooling in her life—but she taught herself Chinese by watching captioned TV dramas and memorizing the pronunciation and structure of the different characters.

YOUR UPLOADS
www.ripleys.com/submit

Tiffany Tezna, from Virginia, and her best friend sent us these pictures of stylish and vibrant wedding and bridesmaid dresses that they designed and constructed from Marshmallow Peeps candy.

Designer Taras Lesko from Covington, Washington, made a scale model of his own head entirely from paper. Taras worked by photographing his head from all sides as a visual guide. He then used computer software to design a three-dimensional model, which is printed out on paper and meticulously assembled into the final giant paper head.

Heads Up

HORSE BLOOD For a 2011 project in Luxembourg exploring trans-species relationships, artist Marion Laval-Jeantet injected herself with horse blood plasma. In the performance piece, titled *May the Horse Live in Me*, she also wore a set of stilts with hooves on the end.

CHOPSTICK TREE To raise awareness of the 100 trees that are felled in China each day to make chopsticks, the China Environmental Protection Foundation assembled 30,000 used chopsticks to create a 16-ft-high (5-m) sculpture of a fallen tree in a Shanghai street.

OCEAN SCULPTURES Artist Andrew Baines stages live "surreal sculptures" in the sea off Australia. In 2011, he persuaded a farmers' group to train a small herd of cows to stand in the ocean for ten minutes so that he could complete his work of art. He had previously posed businessmen reading newspapers in the surf and hired the Adelaide Symphony Orchestra to play tunes in shallow water.

GUN CONVERSION For his work *Palas por Pistolas*, artist Pedro Reyes collected 1,527 guns in the city of Culiacán, Mexico, and transformed them into shovel heads to be used in a tree-planting project.

DORMANT TALENT

Lee Hadwin of Henllan, Wales, has created about 200 pictures, including one that sold for over $150,000... in his sleep. While sleepwalking, Lee—dubbed "Kipasso"—draws on walls, tablecloths, furniture, and newspapers, but the following morning he has no recollection of what he has done. In fact, when awake he displays no artistic talent whatsoever. Now he prepares for his nocturnal wanderings by leaving sketchbooks and charcoal pencils scattered around the house, particularly under the stairs, his favorite workshop.

Sleepwalkers

A sleepwalking expert at the London Sleep Centre in the U.K. has treated people who have driven cars and ridden horses in their sleep. One patient even tried to fly a helicopter. Here are some other bizarre cases:

● **Crane walking** A teenage sleepwalker was rescued in London, England, after being found asleep on the narrow arm of a crane 130 ft (40 m) above ground. She had climbed the crane and walked along the beam while asleep.

● **Cooking with closed eyes** Robert Wood from Fife, Scotland, is such a good chef he can cook while he's asleep! A sleepwalker for more than 40 years, he heads to the kitchen while asleep and, still sleeping, prepares omelets, stir fries, and French fries.

● **Sending e-mails** A 44-year-old woman in the United States sleepwalked to an adjoining room, turned on the computer, connected to the Internet, logged on, and sent three e-mails while asleep. It was only when she received a reply the following day that she realized what she had done.

● **Stepped out of the window** Sleepwalking teenager Rachel Ward stepped out of her bedroom window in West Sussex, England, and plunged 15 ft (4.5 m) to the ground. Although her landing left 6-in (15-cm) divots in the ground, she did not break a single bone.

● **Lawn mowing** U.K. computer engineer Ian Armstrong got out of bed at 2 a.m. and mowed the lawn while naked and fast asleep.

WHALE SONGS Mark Fischer, an expert in marine acoustics from San Francisco, California, captured the sounds of whales and dolphins and transformed their songs into beautifully patterned visual artworks by using a mathematical process known as the wavelet transform.

FILMING EROSION Kane Cunningham bought a clifftop house near Scarborough, England, for a cut-price £3,000 because coastal erosion means that it will soon fall into the sea. He is using it as an art installation, *The Last Post*, rigging rooms with cameras so that he can film its eventual collapse.

ARTWORK CANNED A judge ordered an art storage company from London, England, to pay over £350,000 for accidentally disposing of a sculpture by Indian-born Turner Prize-winning artist Anish Kapoor in a dumpster. The 1984 artwork *Hole and Vessel II* was thrown away during building work in 2004.

HUMAN SPIROGRAPH Illinois-born visual artist Tony Orrico creates huge Spirograph-like artworks using his body as the cog wheel. Holding drawing materials in his hands, he moves his arms in circles while lying straight, bending his knees, or standing on his toes to create patterns on a blank canvas. Each artwork can take 12 hours of physical effort.

VALUABLE VASE An 18th-century Chinese vase found by a brother and sister during a clearout of their late parents' modest semidetached house in London, England, fetched over £51.6 million at an auction in 2010. The auctioneers had given the 16-in-high (40-cm) vase a guide price of only £800,000. When the hammer went down after 30 minutes of frantic bidding, the owners had to be led from the auction room in shock.

STAPLE CITY Artist Peter Root from Guernsey, Channel Islands, built a miniature metropolis from 100,000 staples. His 20 x 10 ft (6 x 3 m) city—named Ephemicropolis—comprised dozens of gleaming silver skyscrapers made from staples and took 40 hours to build.

SMALLEST AQUARIUM Russian microminiature artist Anatoly Konenko has devised the world's smallest aquarium—holding just two teaspoons (10 ml) of water. The miniature glass tank measures 1.2 x 0.9 x 0.6 in (3 x 2.4 x 1.4 cm). Even so, it contains miniature plants, stones, and several tiny zebrafish, which had to be added with a tiny net. The water was applied with a syringe in order to avoid disturbing the aquarium arrangement.

MAGNETIC STATUE Tim Szeto and Denis Saveliev, the founders of Nanodots—small magnetic toy balls—used over 550,000 gold Nanodots to create a replica of the famous Golden Globe award that weighed more than 600 lb (272 kg). The statue was created in Canada before being unveiled in Los Angeles, California.

LEGO FROG Dave Kaleta from Chicago, Illinois, made an anatomically accurate model of a dissected frog from LEGO® bricks. The model took him seven hours to build and used over 1,000 pieces.

HARD TO CREDIT

As a protest against what he considers to be the evil of plastic credit cards, Los Angeles-based artist Cain Motter burns and melts old cards down into creative sculptures, which he then sells for up to $1,200 apiece—to pay off his credit-card bill.

Ripley's **ASK**

Why have you created the story of your persona and background? *The idea came about in a strangely organic way. We knew that we wanted to write some songs together, and we already had come up with the band name "Evelyn Evelyn" through wordplay. One idea led to the next, and all of a sudden we'd created an entire world.*

Why did you pick the conjoined twins angle? Do you have an interest in old-time circus? *Throughout time people have been fascinated by conjoined twins—the idea of having someone so close to you who is a constant confidant and complete companion is both appealing and terrifying to us. As street performers and touring musicians, we have a natural interest in old-time circus, and a lot of our friends are involved in modern circus and new, indie circus. I think the fascination with old-time circus and freak shows is similar. We all, at times, feel like outsiders or freaks.*

How does the story relate to your music? *Well, all of the music in the Evelyn Evelyn project relates in one way or another to their story. We sat down and figured out the twins' biography and let most of the songs rise up out of the events that happened in their life. In some cases it worked the other way around, where we had a song idea and we adjusted their story to incorporate it.*

Does being conjoined restrict your performance and limit your music? *It can be inspiring to have creative limitations, whether those limitations are forced or self-imposed. When performing in costume, it limits us for sure. But that's what is fun about performing these songs. We really have to rethink what we are doing and work together. In a way, it is just like being in a regular band... with the ups and downs and constraints... but different... and weirder. And fun.*

EVELYN ☉ NA⅃ƎVƎ

Dressed identically in connected garments, musical duo Evelyn Evelyn look like conjoined sisters—but in fact they are played by Amanda Palmer and Jason Webley. They even invented a fictional backstory to their characters, claiming that Eva and Lyn Neville were born as conjoined twins on a Kansas farm, sharing between them three legs, two hearts, two arms, three lungs, and a single liver.

® SWEET MUSIC A Japanese fruit company played Mozart to its ripening bananas for a week in the belief that classical music makes for sweeter fruit.

® DOING THE MACARENA A record-breaking total of 2,219 staff and students from schools and colleges in Plymouth, England, simultaneously danced the *Macarena* in July 2011.

® LIFE IMITATING ART While filming his role as the Greek god Achilles in the 2004 movie *Troy*, Brad Pitt tore his left Achilles tendon, delaying the movie's final scenes for months.

® BACKWARD PIANIST U.S. student Evan Petrone can play music with his back to the piano. He filmed himself sitting down, facing away from the keyboard, before twisting his arms into a seemingly impossible position to play "Clocks" by Coldplay. He suffers from Ehlers-Danlos Syndrome, which gives him unusually loose joints and ligaments. He said he chose "Clocks" because it was simple and repetitive, but it still took him more than five hours to get his brain to adjust to his unusual playing position.

® KERMIT COAT For an interview with a German TV station, eccentric U.S. pop singer Lady Gaga wore a coat made from the bodies of *Muppet Show* character Kermit the Frog. The green furry creation by designer Jean-Charles de Castelbajac was draped with dozens of Kermits, and Lady Gaga even wore a Kermit head as a matching hair decoration.

® SOLO SESSION Rajesh Burbure, a professional singer from Nagpur, India, sang continuously for 80 hours—that's more than three days—in 2010, during which time he performed nearly 1,000 songs.

® BACTERIA FASHION Suzanne Lee from the Central Saint Martins School of Fashion and Textiles in London, England, has designed a range of clothes from bacteria. She has developed a technique for creating a cellulose material from a brew of yeast, bacteria, and sweetened green tea, which, when dried, can be shaped into thin shirts and jackets.

HAIR DRESS
Dress designer Thelma Madine and hair stylist Ryan Edwards, both from Liverpool, England, teamed up to create a dress made from 820 ft (250 m) of human hair. It took 300 hours to make, weighs 209 lb (95 kg), and uses hair extensions containing more than 10,000 individual hair wefts. The $75,000 dress also features 1,500 crystals and 12 underskirts.

Dangerous Art

Some artists go to extreme lengths for their work—don't try this at home!

⭐ **Blood Painting** Australian artist Dr. Rev, whose blood painting was featured in *Ripley's Believe It or Not! Strikingly True*, went a step further in 2011. Rev rigged up a 12-gauge shotgun loaded with lead shot, aimed at his own hand placed on a canvas, and pulled the trigger. The result was a great deal of pain and a seriously extreme artwork—a bloody print of his blasted hand.

⭐ **Blasted with Flamethrowers** The art group Interpretive Arson devised a version of the famous Dance Dance Revolution arcade game in which players are blasted with flamethrowers if they get the dance moves wrong. Dance Dance Immolation performers are protected with fireproof suits but the flames that are hurled at them can reach temperatures of almost 3,600°F (2,000°C).

⭐ **Cutting Art** Performance artist Franko B would cut himself in front of an audience and allow himself to bleed freely, losing as much as a pint of blood during each performance and even blacking out. All in the name of art.

⭐ **Branded with Hot Iron** Chinese artist Yang Zhichao had the I.D. number from his passport branded with a hot iron onto his back in a performance in 2000. He has also enlisted doctors to surgically insert soil into his abdomen, and planted grasses into his own skin.

Created by fireworks blasting across paper!

FIREWORK ARTIST

Pyro-artist Rosemarie Fiore from the Bronx, New York, creates unique, abstract paintings in her backyard by exploding fireworks onto blank sheets of paper. She makes eye-catching images with colored smoke bombs, firecrackers, and lasers, bombing the paper a number of times to create layers. Fiore directs the colorful blasts onto paper with buckets, jars, poles, and planks of wood to create a collage effect. The dyes that usually give the aerial explosions their color are then singed across the heavy paper.

Hair Necklace

Artist Kerry Howley from Cambridge, England, makes necklaces from human hair. She spends up to 60 hours creating each necklace, cutting and weaving the strands into abstract shapes. The hair is held in place by tiny specks of glue. Kerry's main source of materials is her mother's Japanese friend, who agreed to have 12 in (30 cm) cut from her waist-length hair.

JUNKYARD GENIUS Retired automobile dismantler Dick Schaefer turns trash into treasure by converting rusty old cars into scary sculptures of monster insects. The yard of his home in Erie, Pennsylvania, houses a giant bee made from a cement truck and a car, as well as a huge spider with the body of a Volkswagen Beetle.

CURTAIN RODS At the Roundhouse venue in London, England, Israeli artist Ron Arad created an installation titled *Curtain Call*—a curtain made of 5,600, 26.5-ft-high (8.1-m) silicon rods. Measuring 59 ft (18 m) in diameter, the curtain formed a 360-degree canvas for screening movies, live performance, or audience interaction.

REGAL FIND A couple renovating their home in Somerset, England, uncovered a 6-ft-high (1.8-m), 500-year-old mural of King Henry VIII on one of the walls. Angie and Rhodri Powell had been removing wooden panels from the wall so that they could paint it. The house was once home to Thomas Cranmer, one of Henry's closest advisers.

LIVER OP U.S. actor Larry Hagman—famous for playing ruthless oil tycoon J.R. Ewing in *Dallas*—has an artwork containing a collection of 150 silver staples from his 1995 liver transplant.

MARTIAL ARTS Sixty-year-old Ba Desheng of Kaifeng City, China, uses kung-fu skills to draw giant calligraphy with a 6-ft-6-in-long (2-m) brush that weighs 11 lb (5 kg).

FOIL BALL Dave Mok of Toronto, Canada, created a 20-lb (9-kg) ball made with tinfoil collected from cigarette pack wrappers over a five-year period.

RICE MOUNTAIN On February 23, 2011, a food company from Shizuoka, Japan, made a rice-ball mosaic of Mount Fuji from 22,350 rice balls in five different colors. The mosaic measured 37 ft 5 in x 21 ft 4 in (11.4 x 6.5 m) and later was dismantled to feed rice balls to some 2,000 people.

RAINING HOUSE For a project conceived by Australian artist James Dive, a fully furnished house in Aarhus, Denmark, was destroyed by raining 44 gal (200 l) of water indoors every minute for a month, causing the onset of damp and dry rot.

UNDER-WATERCOLORS A group of Ukrainian artists specialize in painting underwater at depths of between 6.5 ft and 65 ft (2 m and 20 m) in the Black Sea. All trained scuba divers, they coat their canvasses with a waterproof adhesive before taking the plunge but have just 40 minutes to complete their masterpieces before their oxygen tanks run out.

LARGEST DECK CHAIR Visitors to the beach at Bournemouth, England, in 2012 saw the world's largest deck chair—standing 28 ft (8.5 m) tall, 18 ft (5.5 m) wide, and weighing six tons. It was built by sculptor Stuart Murdoch whose previous works include spending 512 hours creating a life-sized army tank out of 5,016 egg boxes.

DEFYING GRAVITY Artist Adrian Gray, from Dorset, England, creates impressive, gravity-defying sculptures simply by balancing stones on top of each other. He scours his local beach for suitable rocks, boulders, and pebbles and then feels for the balancing point of each stone. He says he does not use any adhesives to keep the stones in place—just hours of his own patience.

MECHANICAL TIGER Tipu, the 18th-century Sultan of Mysore (in modern-day India), commissioned a nearly life-sized mechanical automaton of a tiger mauling a European. The machine included automated movements as well as wails and grunting noises.

PICTURE MOSAIC On December 3, 2011, at Daniel Island, South Carolina, five-year-old Ansley McEvoy and her friends and family—a total of 1,458 people—held poster boards above their heads to create the world's biggest picture mosaic, measuring 81 x 108 ft (24.6 x 33 m). The picture featured Ansley's own drawing of a rainbow.

CHANGING COLORS Surendra Kumar Verma and a team of helpers from Kharagpur, India, created a 294-sq-ft (27-sq-m) Rangoli sand artwork, which appears as two entirely different portraits depending on whether green or red light is used to illuminate it.

ART SICKNESS People with Stendhal Syndrome become so overwhelmed in the presence of fine art that they suffer dizziness, fainting, and confusion.

CABLE HAT To brighten up the dull gray electrical junction boxes in Leeds, England, local artists gave them a makeover. One box was put behind red velvet curtains that opened to reveal a painting of acrobatic rabbits and hares, while another was covered by a giant wooly hat, hand-knitted from electric cable by Sheffield artist Tony Broomhead.

TRASH HOTEL German artist HA Schult built a temporary hotel in Madrid, Spain, from garbage. The five-bedroom Beach Garbage Hotel opened in January 2011.

SCRAP DINOSAUR Brian Boland of Post Mills, Vermont, built "Vermontasaurus," a 25-ft-tall (7.6-m), 122-ft-long (37.2-m) dinosaur sculpture made from wood. He cut a huge pine tree into four pieces and sank them into the ground as the bases for the feet. He assembled the body from old planks and discarded junk, including the belly of an old guitar and part of a ladder from a child's bunk bed.

NOVELTY TREE The Rocks, a shopping district in Sydney, Australia, erected a Christmas tree made from chairs in 2008, another made from bottles in 2009, and one made of bicycles in 2010.

SIDE VIEW The skull image embedded in *The Ambassadors*, a 1533 painting by German artist Hans Holbein the Younger, can only be seen properly when viewed from the side.

BIDDING WAR One of the four versions of Edvard Munch's painting *The Scream* sold at Sotheby's, New York, on May 2, 2012, for $119.9 million—the most ever paid for a work of art at an auction. The iconic picture, painted by the Norwegian artist in 1885, was bought over the phone at the end of a 12-minute bidding war.

BALLET LOVER French artist Edgar Degas (1834–1917) was so fascinated by ballet dancers that he made more than 1,500 paintings, pastels, prints, and drawings of dancers at the Paris-Opera Ballet. Over half of his total works depict dancers.

HUMAN BUG For his sculpture *Ladybug*, Hungarian artist Gabor Fulap created a life-sized human form from 20,000 handmade ladybugs. He made the little beetles from artificial resin, then hand-painted each one individually before applying them so that it looks as if the subject has 20,000 bugs crawling all over her from head to toe.

BALL MOSAIC Volunteers in Toronto, Canada, arranged 1,228 soccer balls to form a 624-sq-ft (58-sq-m) mosaic of the Bank of Montreal logo.

KNIT WIT

Brooklyn-based, Polish-born artist Olek spends hundreds of hours covering cars and even people in crochet. In 2010, she wrapped Wall Street's famous *Charging Bull* sculpture in crochet. In her most ambitious project yet, she has created an entire crocheted living environment. She covered the floors, walls, and all of the furniture in a studio apartment measuring 15 x 14 ft (4.6 x 4.3 m) in bright, acrylic yarn.

CD ART

Fascinated by the way light and color reflect off a compact disk, Sean Avery from Ottawa, Canada, makes sculptures of birds and animals—including a rat and a falcon—from old CDs. He cuts up the disks with scissors, arranges the shards according to size and color, and then attaches them to a wire mesh frame using a hot glue gun. Some of his works use 300 disks and take a month to complete.

ℝ PHOTO MOSAIC In honor of World Sight Day, on October 11, 2012, at Tampa, Florida, eyewear company Transitions Optical created a record-breaking photo mosaic consisting of 176,750 individual photographs and covering an area of 21,479 sq ft (1,995 sq m). People submitted photos of things they would miss seeing if they lost their sight, and the mosaic formed the image of a human eye viewing the world.

ℝ LEGO YODA For Christmas 2011, thousands of San Franciscans built a 12-ft-tall (3.6-m) Santa Yoda, with an ear span of 10 ft (3 m), from about 6,000 LEGO® bricks. The giant model of the *Star Wars* character weighed 4,000 lb (1,816 kg).

ℝ MIRROR WRITING Leonardo da Vinci's personal notes were always written starting from the right side of the page and moving to the left, a technique known as "mirror writing" because anyone who wanted to read his private notebooks had to use a mirror. He only wrote in the standard manner from left to right if he intended his texts to be read by others.

ACKNOWLEDGMENTS

Front cover (t) Courtesy of Olek, (b) Janne Parviainen, www.jannepaint.com; **6–7** Natalie Irish, © air/fotolia.com; **8** (t) Sian Williams, (b) Betfair/Solent News; **9** Wenn.com; **10** (t/l, t/r) Tim Stewart News/Rex Features, (b) © Hideto Nagatsuka/Solent News; **11** (t/l, t/r) Tim Stewart News/Rex Features, (l) Reuters/Cheryl Ravelo, (r) Rex Features; **12** Andrew Lancaster/Rex Features; **13** Gabriel Bouys/AFP/Getty Images; **14** (t/r) © Thomas Launois/Fotolia.com, (t/l) Startraks Photo/Rex Features, (b) Brian Rasic/Rex Features; **15** (t) Nicky J. Sims/Redferns, (c) John Storey/Time Life Pictures/Getty Images, (b) Alex Sudea/Rex Features; **16** Sipa Press/Rex Features; **20** Photographer: Nathan Gallagher; **21** (t) Rob Huibers/Hollandse Hoogte/eyevine, (b/l) Maya Pixelskaya/Rex Features, (b/r) Everett Collection/Rex Features; **22–23** Janne Parviainen, www.jannepaint.com; **24** (t) Rob Matthews, (b) Dario Lopez-Mills/AP/Press Association Images; **25** (t, c) Reuters/Jon Nazca, (b/l) Photographer: M2k Photo model: pink dress: Tiffany Tezna, (b/r) Sipa Press/Rex Features; **26** (t) Taras Lesko (www.visualspicer.com), (b) Lee Hadwin; **27** DC Image Photography; **28** (t) Scott Irvine, (b) Burns!; **29** Courtesy of Voodou, Liverpool; **30** Courtesy of Priska C. Juschka Fine Art, New York; **31** Kerry Howley/Rex Features; **32** Courtesy of Olek; **33** Sean E. Avery;
Back cover Sean E. Avery

Key: t = top, b = bottom, c = center, l = left, r = right, sp = single page, dp = double page

All other photos are from Ripley Entertainment Inc.
Every attempt has been made to acknowledge correctly and contact copyright holders and we apologize in advance
for any unintentional errors or omissions, which will be corrected in future editions.